Animals on the Farm

Turkeys

Aaron Carr

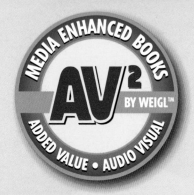

Go to **www.av2books.com**,
and enter this book's
unique code.

BOOK CODE

J239550

AV² by Weigl brings you media
enhanced books that support
active learning.

AV² provides enriched content that supplements and complements this book. Weigl's AV² books strive to create inspired learning and engage young minds in a total learning experience.

Your AV² Media Enhanced books come alive with...

 Audio
Listen to sections of
the book read aloud.

 Video
Watch informative
video clips.

 Embedded Weblinks
Gain additional information
for research.

 Try This!
Complete activities and
hands-on experiments.

 Key Words
Study vocabulary, and
complete a matching
word activity.

 Quizzes
Test your knowledge.

 Slide Show
View images and
captions, and prepare
a presentation.

... and much, much more!

Published by AV² by Weigl
350 5th Avenue, 59th Floor   New York, NY 10118
Website: www.av2books.com   www.weigl.com

Library of Congress Cataloging-in-Publication Data
Carr, Aaron.
Turkey / Aaron Carr.
     pages cm. -- (Animals on the farm)
Audience: K to grade 3.
ISBN 978-1-62127-233-5 (hardcover : alk. paper) -- ISBN 978-1-62127-237-3 (softcover : alk. paper)
1. Turkeys--Juvenile literature. I. Title.
QL696.G27C37 2014
598.6'45--dc23

                              2012044723

Printed in the United States of America in North Mankato, Minnesota
1 2 3 4 5 6 7 8 9 0   17 16 15 14 13

022013
WEP300113

Senior Editor: Aaron Carr   Art Director: Terry Paulhus

Weigl acknowledges Getty Images as the primary image supplier for this title.

Animals on the Farm

Turkeys

CONTENTS

4

I am a small farm animal.
Farmers keep me for food.

5

I am a bird. My body is covered with feathers.

7

I have wings, but I can not fly.
I use my two legs to walk
and run instead.

9

I have red skin over my forehead and beak. This skin is called a snood.

11

I like to eat seeds and bugs. Sometimes, I even eat small lizards.

13

I make a clicking sound to talk with other turkeys. Male turkeys "gobble."

I like to live
with other turkeys.
A group of turkeys
is called a flock.

17

I lay eggs. I sit on the eggs to keep them warm.

My babies hatch from these eggs.

Baby turkeys are called poults. Poults are often kept together to keep them safe and warm.

TURKEY FACTS

These pages provide detailed information that expands on the interesting facts found in the book. These pages are intended to be used by adults to help young readers round out their knowledge of each amazing animal featured in the *Animals on the Farm* series.

Pages 4-5

Farmers keep turkeys for their feathers and meat. Turkeys raised for their meat are called poultry. The turkey is the only poultry bird native to North America. Poultry turkeys grow up to 50 inches (130 centimeters) in length and weigh up to 22 pounds (10 kilograms).

Pages 6–7

Turkeys are birds. There are two kinds of turkeys. Common turkeys are raised for food, while wild turkeys live in nature. The common turkey is larger than the wild turkey and has different feather patterns. The largest recorded turkey weighed 86 pounds (39 kg). Wild turkeys live in hardwood forests and grassy areas.

Pages 8–9

Turkeys have wings but cannot fly. Common turkeys raised on farms are too heavy to fly. The are bred and raised to grow to very large before being sold for meat. Wild turkeys are small enough to fly for short distances. They can fly at speeds up to 55 miles (89 kilometers) per hour for about a quarter of a mile (0.4 km).

Pages 10–11

Turkeys have red skin over their forehead and beak called a snood. More colorful skin, called a wattle, hangs below the turkey's throat. The snood and wattle fill with blood to turn bright red. This helps attract mates. If a turkey is scared, the snood and wattle may turn blue. The snood and wattle become pale if the turkey is sick.

Pages 12–13

Turkeys eat seeds and bugs. Turkeys are omnivores. This means they eat plants and animals. On farms, turkeys are usually fed a mixture of seeds and grains. In nature, turkeys will also eat fruit, insects, and even small reptiles or amphibians, such as salamanders.

Pages 14–15

Turkeys talk by making different kinds of sounds. Female turkeys are called hens. They make a clicking sound. Male turkeys are called toms or gobblers. They make a "gobble" sound. This sound can be heard up to 1 mile (1.6 km) away. Male turkeys often gobble when they hear loud noises and before going to sleep at night.

Pages 16–17

Turkeys like to live with other turkeys. Most common turkeys are kept in special barns to protect them from predators and harsh weather. In nature, turkeys live together in a group called a flock. Within the flock, females and young turkeys stay together in one group, while adult males gather in another group.

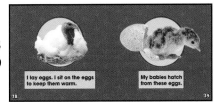

Pages 18–19

Turkeys lay eggs. Their babies hatch from these eggs. Turkey hens lay between 4 and 17 eggs at a time. They sit on all of the eggs to keep them warm until they hatch. However, in most turkey farms, the eggs are kept warm in a special place called a hatchery. Turkey eggs hatch about 28 days after they are laid.

Pages 20–21

Turkey babies are called poults. The first five weeks of a poult's life is called the brooding stage. During this time, farmers keep a close watch on the poults to make sure they are kept warm and well fed. On farms, poults are usually raised to full-grown turkeys in about 20 weeks. They eat more than 65 pounds (30 kg) of food in that time.

KEY WORDS

Research has shown that as much as 65 percent of all written material published in English is made up of 300 words. These 300 words cannot be taught using pictures or learned by sounding them out. They must be recognized by sight. This book contains 42 common sight words to help young readers improve their reading fluency and comprehension. This book also teaches young readers several important content words. These words are paired with pictures to aid in learning and improve understanding.

Page	Sight Words First Appearance	Page	Content Words First Appearance
5	a, am, animal, farm, food, for, I, keep, me, small	5	farmers
6	is, my, with	6	bird, body, feathers
8	and, but, can, have, not, run, to, two, use	8	legs, wings
10	over, this	10	beak, forehead, skin, snood
12	eat, even, like, sometimes	12	bugs, lizards, seeds
15	make, other, sound, talk	15	turkeys
16	group, live, of	16	flock
18	on, them	18	eggs
19	from, these	19	babies
20	are, often, together	20	poults

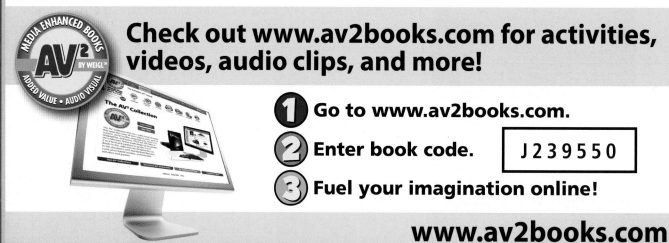